Books by Dennis M Keating

The Olympics:
An Unauthorized Unsanctioned History
*
Charlie Whitman
Was a Friend of Mine
*
Ena Road
*
The Fulda Gap
*
A Chicago Tale
*
Black Lahu
*
Poetry for Men

Charlie Whitman Was a Friend of Mine

The Texas Tower Killer Marine

Dennis M Keating

This book was created by
the Golden Sphere team
in coordination with the Honolulu Guy,
Dennis M Keating

The Author

Dennis M Keating

The Honolulu Guy

DEDICATION

This book is dedicated to all the victims of the Texas Tower Massacre and their families. We honor and recognize the seventeen innocent individuals who were murdered in cold blood by Charlie Whitman. We also honor the many individuals who were shot and injured, and the countless others who suffered heartbreak because they lost family members and friends.

ACKNOWLEDMENTS

Thanks to

**Professor Steven Taylor
Goldsberry
My Mentor**

**Paula Marie Fernandez
and Hikari Kimura
For Artwork and Maps**

**Gail M Baugniet and
Faith Scheideman
Advisors and Proofreaders**

**Sandy
My Wife, Proponent and Ally**

Charlie Whitman
Was a Friend of Mine

The Texas Tower
Killer Marine

A Narrative Poem
written in
Rhyming Couplets

BY

DENNIS M KEATING

Dennis M Keating, the author of **Charlie Whitman Was a Friend of Mine,** has enjoyed a rather peripatetic life. His stories reflect this as each takes place in a different locale – Germany, Thailand, Hawaii, Texas and Chicago.

All five stories are true. Four relate to Keating's personal experiences. The fifth took place almost ninety years ago, but its initial incident occurred just a half block from Keating's current home.

The stories are written for male audiences as they include action, adventure and/or murder in their central themes. They are written in a poetic, rhyming couplet format. Hopefully, this will encourage more men to develop an interest in verse and thereby expand the realm of poetry.

While these tales include gritty elements, many women will also appreciate them. Trustfully, all audiences will find them interesting and compelling.

On August 1, 1966, Charles Whitman was gunned down on the observation deck of the University of Texas Tower in Austin, Texas. In the fourteen hours prior to this, Whitman had shot, knifed and bludgeoned to death seventeen people and injured many more.

Whitman was a former US Marine. Two years prior to the rampage, Whitman served in the Marine Corps at Camp Lejeune, North Carolina.

One of Whitman's fellow Marines at Lejeune was Dennis M. Keating, the author of this story. Whitman and Keating were friends. As a matter of fact, Whitman was the battalion duty clerk, the night Keating was discharged from the Corps. That night, Whitman personally handed Keating his discharge papers. Whitman was the last Marine to whom Keating said goodbye. The two friends never met again.

Keating had been the battalion payroll clerk. Keating got to know Whitman because of this. When Whitman was court martialed, he was demoted. He lost his rank, and lost a large chunk of his pay. As Keating handled Whitman's payroll records, he had to advise Whitman during this critical period. Due to his position, Keating had access to and read Whitman's court martial papers.

Keating still carries the strong impression he had of Whitman from the very first day they met. Keating remembers thinking back then, if he were ever to make a Hollywood feature film about the Marine Corps, he would ask the polite, handsome, and squared away Whitman to play the lead role. At the time, Keating saw Whitman as a true Marine's Marine.

Now, fifty years later, for the first time, Keating tells his personal story about his old friend and fellow Marine, Charlie Whitman, **The Texas Tower Killer.**

Backstory

One evening in early October 1964, just before midnight, I entered the office of the Headquarters Battalion of the 2nd Marine Division at Camp Lejeune, North Carolina, to pick up my discharge papers. The clerk on duty was my friend, Charles Whitman. I signed the papers. We chatted briefly, shook hands and said goodbye. Two hours later I was on an early morning bus to Washington, D.C.

I pretty much forgot about Charlie and my other Marine Corps buddies until twenty-two months later.

On August 1st, 1966. I left my office at the Chicago Police headquarters to catch a subway train home. I bought the evening newspaper; saw Charlie's picture on the front page and read the headline story.

I first met Charlie
through my Marine Corps work.

My MOS,
2nd Marine Division, Payroll Clerk.

I handled the Headquarters Battalion
payroll stuff,

And kept the money
and numbers up to snuff.

I'd just returned from
a Chitown Thanksgiving holiday.

Now, back at Lejeune,
I was computing leatherneck pay.

MOS – Marine Corps term for **Military Occupational Specialty.**

Chitown – A nickname for Chicago

Lejeune – Camp Lejeune, North Carolina, the main Marine Corps base on the east coast of the USA. Lejeune is the home of the 2nd Marine Division.

Leatherneck – A nickname for a Marine

The (Three) Musketeers - Romantic and brave heroes from French literature.

Larry, Moe and Curley - the first names of The Three Stooges, a slapstick comedy trio, popular in the movies and television during the mid-twentieth century.

JFK – **President John F. Kennedy** was assassinated in Dallas on November 22, 1963. His killer was **Lee Harvey Oswald**. Two days later, Oswald was murdered by Jack Ruby, the owner of a sleazy Dallas strip joint.

Who can forget
November '63?

Dallas, Oswald
and Kennedy.

Texas. Marines. Guns.
They're birds of a feather.

Too often, it seems,
they fly together.

Maybe, like the musketeers,
they're an intertwined three.

Ultra-Liberals might say:
more like Larry, Moe, and Curley.

Texas
School Book
Depository
Dallas, Texas

November 22, 1963

Those were not happy times
in the USA.
JFK's death had put a chill
on Thanksgiving Day.

At home in Chicago,
my folks remained sad.

So, being back at Lejeune
kinda made me feel glad.

Shortly after, I met Charlie;
He'd been busted to E-1.

His pay was cut.
Certainly not fun.

Lee Harvey Oswald

Conspiracy theorists claim Oswald was a patsy controlled by others and not a lone assassin. No. Oswald was a stupid, screw up. He was too unreliable to trust.

As a troubled teen, Oswald said *Life Sucks* and joined the Marines. After a troubling time in the Corps, Oswald said *The Marines Suck*, I want to go home and help my Mom. The Marines gave Oswald a *Compassionate Discharge*. Within a few days of arriving home, Oswald said *the USA Sucks, I wanna be a communist and live in Russia*. Oswald moved to Moscow to live his communist dream. In Russia, he publically denounced the USA and told the US Embassy he planned to renounce his US citizenship. TASS, the soviet news agency, loved it; the Marines not so much. As Oswald was still in the Marine Reserves, they said, *You don't wanna be an American? You Suck.* They gave Oswald an *Undesirable Discharge*.

The Ruskies got 15 minutes of PR news from Oswald. They soon realized **Oswald sucked** and was an unstable nut case. They sent him to work in an out of town, factory assembly line. Oswald was crushed. His dream of being an international political Rock Star were shattered. Deeply depressed he attempted suicide. As with other things, he failed. He then returned to the US Embassy singing: **This place Sucks. Please let me go home.**

Back in Texas, no one wanted to hire a rude, arrogant, **Undesirable** Marine. Also, Oswald was obnoxious. Most people disliked him. Previously, he had written to fellow Fort Worther and former **Navy Secretary, John Connally,** begging his discharge be changed to **Honorable**. Oswald didn't get a response. Connally became Governor of Texas. Oswald became furious. **You made my life Suck.** He sought total, bloody revenge at Connally and the military. In April 1963, Oswald tried to shoot former General

Edwin Walker through his dining room window. An easy shot. Oswald missed.

Oswald was **Osvaldovich** to his fellow Marines. A dysfunctional **Shitbird.** A lousy Marine, and a lousy shot. Many Marines believed Oswald was the lone shooter and Governor Connally was his real target. To us, Oswald was a screwed-up dude. He pulled the trigger and missed Connally and caused Kennedy to become unintended collateral damage.

Prior to this, Oswald had opened a post office box for his mail order weapons and ammo. For this, Oswald, a voracious reader, but lousy speller had a pseudonym, **Alek J. Hidell**. His adjusted anagram for **Jekyll/Hyde**, the good/evil character with a duel personality, created by the author, Robert Lewis Stevenson. Oswald had a kinship with the troubled, psychologically frustrated Dr. Jekyll. For the dysfunctional Oswald, his inexact anagram was clever. **I'm a genius. The world sucks for not seeing my greatness.**

Most grunts who got busted
were screwed-up dudes,

Full of anger at the Corps
and hateful attitudes.

We called 'em Shitbirds,
Pitiful, short-circuited dopes.

They'd lost their self-respect;
Along with their hopes.

These demoted losers yelled at me,
As I tried my best.

They were hurting bad inside,
And now they were paid less.

Jarhead – Nickname for a Marine

E-1 – A private. The lowest rank, in the Marines.

Grunt – Nickname for a Marine.

Shitbird – A nickname for a screwed up, f*cked up Marine.

Squared Away – A well-organized, neat and disciplined Marine. Similar to being combat efficient, all Marines are required to be squared away at all times. Often, those Marines who are reduced in rank to the lowest level, E-1, simply give up and no longer cared. They know it is just a matter of time, before the Marines kick them out for good.

I anticipated
An angry jarhead facing me.

This was not true for Charlie.
He was polite as he could be.

His uniform was neatly pressed
And spotlessly clean.

Nodding with respect,
Here stood a Squared Away Marine.

We worked out his payroll math
For an hour that day.

His wife's benefits were cut sharply
Due to his decreased pay.

Court Martial - A military trial that determines if a Marine is guilty of a crime. If so, a punishment is then determined. A court marital does not mean expulsion from the military. In Charlie's case, he was demoted in rank and served a certain punishment time. He then was brought in once again as a full Marine.

The Uniform Code of Military Justice allows for lesser forms of punishment than a court martial for minor violations of military law. During his tour of duty, the author often saw higher-ups look the other way, or mete out much lesser punishments for the same infractions that Charlie Whitman was found guilty.

Been had – Cheated or falsely set up. Charlie's situation is comparable to the scene in the film *Casablanca*, when Captain Renault is shocked to find gambling in Rick's Casino.

That next month, Charlie came back
More than twice.

He showed no visible anger.
He was always polite and nice.

In Charlie's files, his court martial
Papers caught my eye.

I read them one night
After bidding him goodbye.

What I read baffled me.
I felt Charlie had been had.

His three so-called crimes
Were simply nothing bad.

SOP - Standard Operating Procedure. In slang usage, SOP means something that is very common or always happens.

Russian Roulette - A dangerous game played with a loaded pistol. The shooter holds a revolver to his side after placing a single bullet in one of the cylinder's six chambers. The cylinder is spun; the pistol is raised to the head and the trigger is pulled.

In our Marine Corps unit, the guys played several modified and safer versions of Russian Roulette. In one version, the shooter held his arm down at his side, so he could quickly glance to see if a bullet was in a visible chamber. If he took too much time looking, he was labeled a **Chicken** or a coward. His speed at bringing the pistol up to his head and pulling the trigger was considered a gauge of his bravery and manliness.

I pondered the words I read,

And couldn't figure them out.

After all, this is the Marine Corps
We're talking about.

Busted for gambling. What?
Are you kidding me?

In the Corps,
Friday night poker games were S.O.P.

Busted for an extra weapon.
A hip pocket gun.

Give me a break.
Half the enlisted packed one.

In our second version of Russian Roulette, the shooter pointed a revolver at a target person. The target person said to fire or not fire. Then, the shooter pulled the trigger. If the target said not to fire and there was no bullet in the chamber, the target person was labeled a **Chicken**. Nineteen-year-old Marines do not like to be called **Chicken**.

The author knew of several incidents of guys getting wounded and was present at one incident that was covered up.

15 for 20 – Giving a loan of $15.00 and collecting $20.00 a few days later. During the 1960's, the Marines lined up and were paid in cash. The payroll clerk would get back his loan and interest immediately when the Marine was handed his money. Often, payroll clerks were paid on Fridays and the rest of the Marines on Monday. This allowed payroll clerks to give out weekend loans and make interest money from the loans.

In our payroll office,
On any weekend day,

Our version of Russian Roulette
Was the in game to play.

Who was a chicken?
Who was not?

Naturally, sometimes,
A guy did get shot.

We'd just patch up the wounds
And hide all the facts,

And keep the details hidden
From the higher-ups' backs.

C.O. – The Commanding Officer of a Marine company. Normally, a company C.O is a Captain who commands up to 200 members.

Louie – Or Luey or Lewey – A slang term for either a Second Lieutenant or a First Lieutenant ranks Officers start as Second Lieutenants. After satisfactory time and performance, they are promoted to First Lieutenants. Later, they are promoted to Captain. These are Company Level Ranks.

Battalions usually consist of five or six companies and have field grade officers: Majors, Lieutenant Colonels and Colonels.

Battalion officers conduct court martials. The author believes a company level officer must have convinced a battalion officer that Charlie's minor infractions warranted a court marital trial, rather than the more normal, lesser judicial procedure. The author's attempts to uncover the backstory were unsuccessful.

Busted for lending money
With interest! That's a crime?

We payroll clerks
Did it all the time.

We'd pay ourselves early
Before the weekend;

Then offer 15 for 20,
To grunts eager to spend.

To me, this court martial thing
really stank.

Some officer had it in for Charlie,
One who had a bit of rank.

CAMP LEJEUNE
HOME OF
EXPEDITIONARY
FORCES IN READINESS

Sign at the entrance of Camp Lejeune,
North Carolina.

I figured his C.O. pushed it,
While trying to guess who.

A 2nd or 1st Louie couldn't
shove this garbage through.

Due to Charlie's payroll issues,
He became a casual friend.

I really liked the guy
And hoped he'd mend.

If we met on the street,
I'd always stop and chat.

At least a "How's it going?"
And other stuff like that.

He'd earned back a Stripe - He'd been promoted back to a former rank. In Charlie's case, he had started, as all enlisted Marines do, as a Private (E-1). During his career, he had risen to Lance Corporal (E-3). His court martial trial reduced him back to the basic enlisted rank of (E-1), a rank that has no stripes on its uniform's arm. At the time of our last meeting, Charlie had started to move back up again and had recently become a Private First Class (E-2).

Life moved forward
Until October '64.

My time was up.
I was done with the Corps.

With bags packed heavy
and my spirits light,

I was happy to see
Charlie on duty that night.

He'd earned back a Stripe.
He was turning out to be real.

Good goin', Charlie Boy.
We both know you got a raw deal.

PERSONAL DATA	1. LAST NAME - FIRST NAME - MIDDLE NAME KEATING, Dennis Michael	2. SERVICE NUMBER 2017958	3A. GRADE, RATE OR RANK LCpl (E-3)	b. DATE OF RANK (Day, Month, Year) 1 August 1964

4. DEPARTMENT, COMPONENT AND BRANCH OR CLASS U.S. MARINE CORPS RESERVE	5. PLACE OF BIRTH (City and State or Country) Chicago, Cook, Illinois	DATE OF BIRTH	DAY 07	MONTH Aug	YEAR 40

7 a. RACE Caucasian	b. SEX Male	c. COLOR HAIR Brown	d. COLOR EYES Blue	e. HEIGHT 66"	f. WEIGHT 137	8. U.S. CITIZEN ☐ YES ☐ NO	9. MARITAL STATUS Single

10 a. HIGHEST CIVILIAN EDUCATION LEVEL ATTAINED College-4	b. MAJOR COURSE OR FIELD BusAdmin

TRANSFER OR DISCHARGE DATA	11 a. TYPE OF TRANSFER OR DISCHARGE Transfer to Marine Corps Reserve	b. STATION OR INSTALLATION AT WHICH EFFECTED Camp Lejeune, North Carolina			

c. REASON AND AUTHORITY #202 Expiration of Enlistment Auth para 13258 Marine Corps Personnel Manual & Marine Corps Order 1900.25	EFFECTIVE DATE	DAY 07	MONTH Oct	YEAR 64

12. LAST DUTY ASSIGNMENT AND MAJOR COMMAND ServCo, HqBn, 2dMarDiv	13 a. CHARACTER OF SERVICE HONORABLE	b. TYPE OF CERTIFICATE ISSUED DD Form 217MC

SELECTIVE SERVICE DATA	14. SELECTIVE SERVICE NUMBER N/A	15. SELECTIVE SERVICE LOCAL BOARD NUMBER, CITY, COUNTY, STATE N/A		16. DATE INDUCTED DAY MONTH YEAR N/A	

17. DISTRICT OR AREA COMMAND TO WHICH RESERVIST TRANSFERRED 9th MARCORDIST, 601 Hardesty Ave., Kansas City, Missouri

SERVICE DATA	18. TERMINAL DATE OF RESERVE OBLIGATION DAY 28 MONTH Jun YEAR 68	19. CURRENT ACTIVE SERVICE OTHER THAN BY INDUCTION a. SOURCE OF ENTRY ☒ ENLISTED(First Enlistment) ☐ ENLISTED(Prior Service) ☐ REENLISTED ☐ OTHER	b. TERM OF SERVICE (Years) 2	c. DATE OF ENTRY DAY 08 MONTH Oct YEAR 62

20. PRIOR REGULAR ENLISTMENTS None	21. GRADE, RATE OR RANK AT TIME OF ENTRY INTO CURRENT ACTIVE SERVICE Private	22. PLACE OF ENTRY INTO CURRENT ACTIVE SERVICE (City and State) Chicago, Cook, Illinois

23. HOME OF RECORD AT TIME OF ENTRY INTO ACTIVE SERVICE	24. STATEMENT OF SERVICE	YEARS	MONTHS	DAYS
	a. NET SERVICE THIS PERIOD		00	00
	b. OTHER SERVICE		06	10
	c. TOTAL ACTIVE SERVICE		06	10
25. SPECIALTY NUMBER AND TITLE 0142 Disbursing Man 0142 Disbursement Clerk	d. FOREIGN AND/OR SEA SERVICE	00	00	00

26. DECORATIONS, MEDALS, BADGES, COMMENDATIONS, CITATIONS AND CAMPAIGN RIBBONS AWARDED OR AUTHORIZED

27. WOUNDS RECEIVED AS A RESULT OF ACTION WITH ENEMY FORCES

28. SERVICE SCHOOLS OR COLLEGES, COLLEGE TRAINING COURSES AND/OR POST-GRADUATE COURSES SUCCESSFULLY COMPLETED			
SCHOOL OR COURSE	DATES (From - To)	MAJOR COURSES	COURSES SUCCESSFULLY COMPLETED
None	None	Spanish I East Carolina College	None

VA DATA	30 a. GOVERNMENT LIFE INSURANCE IN FORCE ☐ YES ☒ NO	b. AMOUNT OF ALLOTMENT N/A	c. MONTH ALLOTMENT DISCONTINUED N/A

31. VA BENEFITS PREVIOUSLY APPLIED FOR (Specify type) N/A	b. VA CLAIM NUMBER C- N/A

AUTHENTICATION	32. REMARKS Recommended for reenlistment Good Conduct Medal Period commences 8Oct62(1stAwd) No time lost current enlistment No periods in an excess leave status Lump sum leave settlement paid for 00 days unused leave Social Security Number

33. PERMANENT ADDRESS FOR MAILING PURPOSES AFTER TRANSFER OR DISCHARGE (Street, RFD, City, County and State) 5908 W. Eastwood Ave., Chicago, Illinois	34. SIGNATURE OF PERSON BEING TRANSFERRED OR DISCHARGED *Dennis Michael Keating*
35 a. TYPED NAME, GRADE AND TITLE OF AUTHORIZING OFFICER W. L. MATTMILLER, Capt., USMC GO	b. SIGNATURE OF OFFICER AUTHORIZED TO SIGN *W. L. Mattmiller*

DD FORM 1 NOV 55 214	REPLACES EDITION OF 1 JUL 52, WHICH IS OBSOLETE.	ARMED FORCES OF THE UNITED STATES REPORT OF TRANSFER OR DISCHARGE	1

A DD 214, the standard Discharge Paper.

I cheered silently
and gave him congrats.

Happy to see a PFC had bested
A scumbag officer rat.

Charlie gave me my discharge

And noted my happy glow.

We talked of what I'd do,

and where I'd go.

We chatted some more
and then, when through,

Shook hands, and Charlie said,
"God be with you!"

Congrats - Congratulations

PFC - Private First Class

Scumbag – Slang for someone who is viewed as contemptible.

I never thought I'd see
Charlie's face again.

Then, some two years later,
on a Chicago subway train,

The front-page news splash
was clear to see.

Charlie's easy-going smile
was looking straight at me.

The story noted
The hot summer day.

Austin, Texas in August?
Sure, it's always that way.

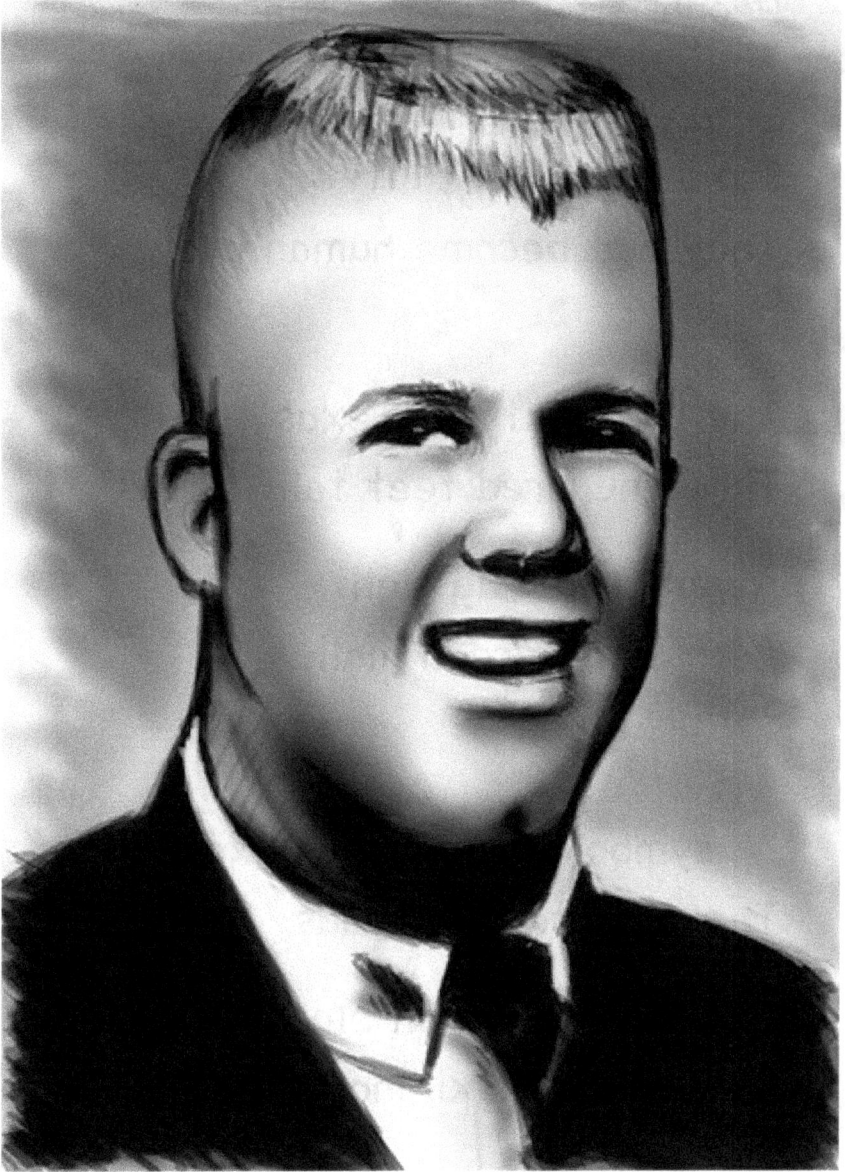

People sitting in the sun;
Children at play.

Totally unaware
They had become human prey.

The University of Texas Tower,
Three hundred feet tall.

A very imposing sight
Across the green mall.

"A symbol of Academic Excellence,"
The website now reads.

It doesn't mention bloody bodies
Or a Marine's killing deeds.

When the first shot rang out,
No one bothered to look.

They were napping,
Idly chatting, or reading a book.

The first student, a co-ed, fell.
No one looked around.

Her boyfriend asked, "What's wrong?"
As she hit the ground.

Those few words
were the last he ever said.

A few seconds later,
He was down, bloody and dead.

Next killed: a Ph.D.,
A visiting professor of math.

Picked off on the South Mall.
He didn't count on that.

A Marine sharpshooter.
A high tower and a 360° view.

Picking off marks was easy.
Like shooting hippos in a zoo.

A Remington 700 rifle
With a sniper scope.

Targets within 300 yards
Had no hope.

Emergency!

Emergency!

A police switchboard operator

Fear filled people's faces.
Some uncontrollably cried.

A few more bang-bangs.
Everyone scurried to hide.

Flooded with uncertainty.
Which way to go?

What's happening?
There was no way to know.

Just minutes into it,
the police phone started to ring.

"Hurry to campus!
It's all crazy. Someone's shooting!"

That ain't Shootin'

That's

Marine Corps Shootin'

An individual ducking for cover

More calls went out.
"We need every cop in town."

"Emergency! Emergency!"
"Another body down."

Young Patrolman Speed
was the first cop to arrive.

Speed wasn't fast enough.
Bang-bang. He was no longer alive.

Then a few gutsy officers
Reached the tower base.

All held stoic looks. They knew
The danger they'd faced.

For ninety minutes, Whitman shot at and killed strangers who were walking at or near the University of Texas. After a short time, he was confronted by return fire from numerous weapons carried by various citizens of Texas who were in the area. Do you know how many Central Texas Good Ol' Boys carry weapons in their pickup truck?

Up the elevator, they peered
Cautiously out the door.

Their quick glances saw bloody bodies
sprawled on the floor.

One cop signals,
You go left; we go right.

One crossed himself. He knew
This would be a death fight.

Fortune sided with the police.
Charlie was caught by surprise.

Hardly a second to react
When he saw their eyes.

Blam!
Blam!
Blam!

A gun

A pistol rang out,
Then a shotgun.

Blam! Blam! Blam!
Charlie was done.

The total tally?
Some 17 dead,

Thirty plus transported
to a hospital bed.

During the next few hours
Things quieted down.

During the next few months,
Charlie was the talk of the town.

One Shot

One Kill

A Marine Corps Tradition

TV anchors watched
as their ratings shot high.

Just like JFK's death, there were
Theories and questions of why.

America's first mass murder
in nearly ten years.

All wrapped up by Prime Time.
Media barons gave cheers.

For corporate networks,
It was nice, clean, and tight.

Ad revenues went up by airing
A new detail every night.

Clutter Farmhouse - This refers to the nonsensical killing of the Clutter family in small town Iowa in November 1959. Initially, the crime received little national news coverage. Six years later, at the end of 1965, the author, Truman Capote, published the book, **In Cold Blood**.

In Cold Blood, presented a detailed account of the killing; the killers, and the victims. The book became a bestseller just months before the Texas Tower killings. This book made many publishers and media executives realize they could make money from the public's fascination with sensational killings.

This Texas Tower Massacre
was a really visual deal.

Not like the Clutter Farmhouse
In a remote Kansas field.

The news bosses realized
for a month or two

That any new fact or twist
meant extra revenue.

A Texas Tower pic could catch
more eyeballs on the 10 PM news

Than a bikini-clad gal
dishing out free booze.

Requiescat In Pace

A Catholic Priest

Now, 50 years have passed.
Still, many questions remain.

Perhaps more will come,
With more theories to explain.

What factors make a mass killer
Out of an average Joe?

Childhood beatings? Brain tumor?
We'll never actually know.

Now, when driving on I-35,
Down Austin way,

I say a silent prayer
For those poor souls killed that day.

Semper Fi

Semper Fi – Always Faithful. The Marine Corps greeting.

Semper Fi - The shortened form of the Latin phrase, **Semper Fidelis**, the motto of the US Marine Corps. In English, **Semper Fidelis** means **Always Faithful.**

Then, one more for my fellow Marine,
As I look to the sky.

"God be with you, Charlie!"

And yes, **"Semper Fi."**

University of Texas

24th St

The Drag - Guadalupe St

Speedway

**University of Texas
Main Campus**

Littlefield Fountain

21st St

Murder Victims of Charlie Whitman

Family Members

Margaret Whitman – Charlie Whitman's mother. Killed in her home.

Kathy Whitman - Whitman's wife. Killed in their home.

Killed inside the Texas Tower

Edna Townsley - A Tower receptionist.

Martin Gabour - A Tower visitor. A service station manager.

Marguerite Lamport - A Tower visitor. A housewife.

Killed on the University campus

Baby Boy Wilson - Shot in the womb of his six-month pregnant mother, Claire Wilson, Claire survived the shooting.

Patrolman Billy Speed - The first Austin police officer to respond to the massacre.

Robert Boyer - A visiting mathematics professor.

Thomas Ashton - A Peace Corps trainee.

Thomas Eckman - A UT student.

Roy Schmidt - A city electrician.

David Gunby - A UT student. Gunby required ongoing dialysis treatment for thirty-five years. Finally, in 2001, because of the ongoing pain, Gunby chose to stop the dialysis. He died a few days later.

Killed in the Guadalupe Street area

Karen Griffith - A high school student.

Thomas Karr - A UT student.

Claudia Rutt - A recent high school graduate.

Paul Sonntag - A recent high school graduate.

Harry Walchuk - A UT graduate student.

The Aftermath

Shortly after the Texas Tower killings, Texas Governor John Connally ordered an investigation into the incident and into the perpetrator, Charles Whitman.

One month later, in September 1966, the Connally Commission issued a report entitled: ***Medical Aspects of the Charles J. Whitman Catastrophe.*** The report stated Whitman did have a **brain tumor**, but the commission could not determine with clarity the tumor's impact on Whitman's mental state.

Also noted was Whitman's hostility toward his father. This related to the **terrible domestic abuse** Whitman, his siblings and his mother suffered under his nasty and evil, control freak father.

The author believes both issues played major roles in the killings.

Charlie's Family

Charlie's father, C. A. Whitman, Jr. was the epitome of a physically and mentally abusive husband and father. C. A. believed he had the right to punch out and psychologically devastate his wife and children regularly for any disagreement or minor shortcoming. He always demanded excellence from his children, and, he used physical abuse if they fell short of the unrealistic goals he set for them.

Until his death, C.A. lived in total denial concerning his domestic violence crimes against his wife and children. His main pride was a collection of sixty guns that included two machine guns.

Less than 90 days after his wife was buried, C.A. remarried. His new wife, 23, had a 3-year-old son. The marriage lasted just a few weeks, with the divorce related to C.A. severely beating her son.

C.A. quickly married again for a third time to the mother of the wife of his son, John. This marriage lasted longer than the second marriage, but was continually marred by C.A.'s violent rages.

Charlie's mother, Margaret Whitman, was the textbook example of the Battered Wife Syndrome. In May 1966, less than three months before Charlie's killing rampage, Margaret worked up the courage to leave her long abusive husband and their home in Florida. Charlie drove to Florida to bring his mother to Austin to live near him.

Charlie's youngest brother, John, at age 18, got married within a year of the Texas Tower killings. He was killed in a barroom fight in 1973 at age 24. His widow later died as a heroin addict.

Charlie's other brother, Patrick, married at age 20, a year before the Tower killings. In 1973, around the time his brother, John, was killed, Patrick announced to his wife that he was gay. He chose to move out of their home and move to California. He died of AIDS while living in Los Angeles.

God be with you!

ABOUT THE AUTHOR

Dennis M Keating has enjoyed a peripatetic lifestyle. His international perspective and eclectic enthusiasm for life come from his forty some years in Germany; Thailand; China and Hawaii.

For the last ten years, Keating and his wife, Sandy, have been living a quiet life in Waikiki. Normally, he can be found pounding his iMac keyboard, hiking the Diamond Head trail, or strolling with his wife at sunset along the sands of Waikiki.

Keating writes on a diverse range of topics. His books draw upon his multifarious interests and personal experiences. Most of his books are nonfiction.

Keating's Facebook page:
https://www.facebook.com/TheHonoluluGuy/
He is happy to Friend you on Facebook.
In 2016, Keating released - *The Olympics:*

An Unauthorized Unsanctioned History

In 2017, Keating released
Poetry for Men - Action Adventure Murder is a compilation of Keating's five poetry books.

Charlie Whitman was a Friend of Mine. The story of the Texas Tower Killer.

Ena Road. Murder and racism in Hawaii.

The Fulda Gap. A Cold War confrontation.

A Chicago Tale. A triple murder story.

Black Lahu. Opium, life and death in the Golden Triangle.

His email is **lostpuka@gmail.com**
His websites are:
GoldenSphere.com & **HonoluluGuy.com**

Keating owns all rights to the material in this book. For film rights, or for other reasons, please contact him.

www.ingramcontent.com/pod-product-compliance
Lightning Source LLC
Chambersburg PA
CBHW050602280326
41933CB00011B/1945